PART 1

THE INFINITE
RULES TO MONEY

LISA LEE HAIRSTON

Order this book online at www.trafford.com
or email orders@trafford.com

Most Trafford titles are also available at major online book retailers.

All Scriptures mentioned throughout this book are taken from the King James
Version and The Amplified Version of the Bible unless otherwise noted!!!

Printed in the United States of America.

ISBN: 978-1-4907-2790-5 (sc)
ISBN: 978-1-4907-2789-9 (e)

Trafford rev. 02/11/2014

 www.trafford.com

North America & international
toll-free: 1 888 232 4444 (USA & Canada)
fax: 812 355 4082

Contents

Dedication Page

I dedicate this book to Jehovah God—A God who is so Infinite that He makes a Centillion dollars (1 with 303 Zeroes) look like pocket change!!!

I also dedicate this book to every individual who dares to set a new course in life by seeing *Infinite Money and The Infinite Rules To Money* in ways it has never been viewed before by anyone.

I wish you *Godspeed* as you develop *The Perfect Money Psychology* that you may only be hearing about for the first time!!! But, then again, my ministry is to reveal that which may never be addressed by anyone else, yet needs to be heard none the less!

It has been my experience that most individuals who disregard *The Infinite Rules To Money* and dismiss them as nothing more than wishful thinking employ these rules on a negative spectrum in spite of themselves, which only reinforces in my mind the notion that *The Infinite Rules To Money* will work if used correctly as God Intended.

May God Richly Bless You!!! And May God Continually Reveal To You Just How Much Money Currently Exists For You In the Spirit Realm That Is Just waiting for you to discover <u>and</u> unleash into your Life!!!

The Half Is Yet To Be Told About How Astronomically Wealthy You Are At This Particular Moment!!! Anything LE$$ Is Totally Unacceptable To God!!!

Happy Reading!!!
Lisa Lee Hairston

Acknowledgements

I would like to take this time to acknowledge each and every family member, without whom, this book would most definitely not be possible!!!

Foreword

Losing two paragraphs of my original foreword, I questioned whether I should retype the foreword later, or rewrite a whole new draft. I got an immediate answer. As I put the final touches on this book, making sure that every word that needed to be said was in order before I submitted the manuscript to my publisher, I came under heavy satanic attack that just seemed to come out of nowhere. It was almost as if satan was doing everything in his power to make sure that *The Infinite Rules To Money* did not make it into your hands.

The same has held true for the past three years as I attempted to type the words contained within these pages. Each time I got to the point where I could make great leaps in starting the book, I would get sick for several months and could not finish typing the words I had written down on paper.

As I submitted this manuscript to the publisher's today, I was not at all happy with the layout of what I had worked so diligently on for years. This was the first time in my career as a published author that I submitted any kind of draft that was not up to my highest standards.

But according to Romans 8:28, "All things work together for good to them who love the Lord, who are the called according to His purpose." My testimony, which was included in the original Foreword as to how I actually ended up studying *The Infinite Rules To Money*, was only reinforced.

The story of my life is that from 2004 to 2008, I was unemployed, and despite every effort to find a job, nothing came to fruition. This book is the result of how powerful the *Infinite Rules To Money* actually are, especially when it seems as if every door that I expected to go through financially was deliberately, purposefully, intentionally, calculatingly, and knowingly shut closed in my face.

Lastly, as the Title of this book, *The Infinite Rules To Money—Part 1* suggests, there will be a Part 2, and a Part 3, and a Part 4, if not more. In Part 2, *The Infinite Rules To Money* will go into greater Spiritual detail as to why *Infinite Money is looking* for you!!!

Happy Reading!!! I am looking forward to seeing you in the *Trillionaire Club!!!*

Rule # 1: Money Always Goes Where It Is Preached!

The Spirit of the Lord is upon me, because He hath anointed me to preach the Gospel to the poor; He hath sent me to heal the brokenhearted, to preach deliverance to the captives, and recovering of sight to the blind, to set at liberty them that are bruised, to preach the acceptable year of the Lord (Luke 4:18).

The number one rule to money is that you cannot have a lot of money if you refuse to say the right things about money. You cannot talk broke and expect to become rich! It is absolutely impossible to talk rich and stay broke! You cannot reach the palace talking like a peasant. You cannot talk like a loser and become a winner. What you say about money, and what you say when you talk about money, on a regular and consistent basis, will determine how much money you will attract into your life.

This rule is the number one reason I decided to put *The Infinite Rules To Money* into manuscript form. This is the number one rule people always violate. All the time, I have people who tell me, "I am not going to say I have money if I do not have it. That would be lying. If I do not have it, I just do not have it. I might as well tell the truth!"

The truth of the matter is that these people who make such a bold statement in such a proud manner will never have as much money as the people who dare to say, "I have a lot of money." Yet, these individuals who refuse to follow *The Infinite Rules To Money* correctly are always the first ones to call you everything but a Child of God when you dare to "call those things that be not as though they were."

In the early 1990's, I was attending college, and I experienced math anxiety during each quiz or exam. No matter how well I knew the material, as soon as the professor said, "Time," or "You have ten minutes left," I would have a panic attack, after which I could not remember how to perform the simplest thing on the test. I continued experiencing this anxiety during each math exam or quiz until I found a technique to counteract it.

Every day after I got home from school, I would say to myself over and over out loud, "I have plenty of time." As a result, I lost my anxiety completely. I could always complete the quiz or exam with time to spare. I aced each math test with flying colors.

It dawned on me that I could use this same principle to attract money, even if and when I did not have a dime in my pocket. I would just repeat these words to myself millions of times a day, **"I have plenty of money!"** If I doubted my own words concerning having plenty of money, all I had to do was remind myself that this principle worked 100% of the time, each time I said, "I have plenty of time!!!

The more I said, "I have plenty of money," the more money I attracted!!! The problem came in when others became offended when they witnessed my increase in money. I had stepped into a never-ending, eternal and perpetual overflow of money no one could understand. I had become my own Money Preacher! I had deliberately chosen to say all the right things about money.

Whereas others were saying, "I am not going to say I have money if I do not have money," I was saying, "I am not going to say I am broke, even if I do not have a penny in my pocket. Regardless of how much money I had at the moment, I kept on saying, **"I have money and more money is coming!"** And that money just kept on coming!!!

When such negativity arises when you begin to say the right things about money, welcome that opportunity to strengthen your resolve and fortitude. If someone can make you feel badly because you are a money magnet, you will start to believe that you do not deserve to have money, which we will discuss later.

Never apologize for having money!!! And never feel badly when you do have money. People will talk about you if you have $1 or $100 Trillion, so you might as well talk yourself into having the $100 Trillion! Give them something positive to talk about!!!

Rule # 2: Money Always Goes Where It Is Heard!

So then faith cometh by hearing, and hearing by the word of God (Romans 10:17).

I used to always ask myself why everyone I knew went out of their way to talk me out of having lots of money. I could not figure out why they had a problem with the very idea of my having an over abundance of money. The more I talked about money, the more others refused to even discuss the topic of money when I came into their immediate space. They would say, "I do not want to talk about money."

These individuals either had money, but did not want me to have it, or they did not want to take the time out of their busy schedules to talk themselves into having lots of money. They did, however have plenty of time to tell me twenty-five million reasons why I should not have money, which is a major violation of The *Infinite Rules To Money!!!*

The time it takes for anyone to remind you why money is not important is valuable time that particular person could have used to follow *The Infinite Rules To Money!!!* If I had just one penny for every time someone said, "Money is not everything, I would be a Zillionaire a Zillion times over.

Then, it dawned on me why people were avoiding the topic of money. Imagine sitting in a room with one million employees and your boss gives everyone in the room a raise and a promotion except you, although he or she knows you are worthy of such a raise and promotion. They either tell you "Your time will come," or "God is not going to give you something you are not ready for."

At first you believe such nonsense until you wake up to the reality that if you put all the 999,999 employees together, they still could not equal your sole performance, and they know it. The problem is that you

3

were not supposed to know it. They did not want you to know that "You were all that!!!!!" You are all that and more!!!

The bottom line is that if you ever find yourself on the receiving end of such an extreme example, which I have always been on the receiving end of, you were never supposed to hear anything about money. The assumption is that you would have what you had heard.

In fact, there are people out there, many of whom you know, who would rather for anyone to hear about money than you. Why? These individuals think you would end up with more money than what they had!!! And they were hoping you would not hear with either your physical ears or your spiritual ear, all the money you would be coming into.

This is the second most important reason I wrote this book—to put you in a position to hear about the money you are not expected to hear about or have. I am a Money Preacher! My Assignment is money and I am on Assignment right now by giving you this information.

It took years for me to discover these money principles that have been in existence since the beginning of time. Once I uncovered *The Infinite Rules To Money,* it took me at least two years to believe the principles worked. My objective is to pass my knowledge on to you so that you will not have to spend ten or more years trying to find out what was so readily available, but not discussed openly due to someone else's fear that you might become wealthy.

Read the Bible from cover to cover and you will see that it is saturated with wealth and money that has yet to be tapped into. My job as a Money Preacher is to help you see money in places others refuse to look.

Remember the scenario about you being passed over for a raise and promotion? There is one important fact you must take to heart immediately:

High Self-Worth = High Financial Worth!

The more worthy you become in your own mind first, the wealthier you become financially. Everyone around you is trying to cut off your self-worth before you get the money, so you will not have as much money as you are actually worth—which is priceless!!! They will try to convince you that you are not smart enough, or beautiful enough, or tall enough, or wealthy enough to attract *Infinite Wealth* or *Infinite Money*. Then you feel a need to run out and get more education, more beauty, and more money before you can become as wealthy as you want to be. Nothing can be further from the truth.

Get your Money Mentality Right first—to the point where you know without a doubt that having lots of money is your destiny. When you can see yourself in your mind having all the money your heart desires, everything else in your life will automatically fall into place with no effort at all, except for taking the time to say the right things about money in the face of those who will not. Work is not really work when you are having so much fun doing that work!!!

Every time anyone tells you why you of all people could never have money, say a silent "Thank you." That is God's way of telling you that you are next in line for the money you are not expected to have, and that you should be aware that someone thinks you will have more money than they would ever have, in half the time.

Throughout this book, I will absolutely tell you things about money that no one else would want you to know. That is my trademark—to share with you pertinent information no one would dare tell you. And what you need to know is that no secure person in his or her right mind would ever want for you to be ignorant concerning the laws or the rules to money.

Only an insecure person would go out of the way to block your great financial money flow. I am going out of my way to tell you that you have great financial substance and you are more financially stable than you know!

I spent too many years seeking out *The Infinite Rules To Money* on my own to allow anyone's negativity, greed, selfishness, or ignorance concerning money to bring me down to a lesser standard of thinking about that money. The truth about money is that there is a level of money that is yet to be tapped into, even by those in the top 1% of the income bracket, and that level of money *has no respecter of persons.*

Unlike some people, money is an Equal Opportunity Thinker which cannot wait to find its way to those who will take the time to master *The Infinite Rules To Money.* Believe it or not, that includes you! And that fact will become more embedded into your psyche if you continue reading, studying, and applying these *Infinite Rules To Money.*

The most important fact about this significant rule is that you are what you hear on a regular basis! You really do become what you hear if you hear it long enough. That is why I will always walk away from negative speaking individuals who deliberately or unknowingly insist on speaking poverty into my spirit to keep me in the wrong, incorrect, and improper mode of thinking about money.

Surround yourself around rich thinking people who are always talking the right money language. If you cannot find any such people, find a quiet place where you can be alone daily so that you can deliberately say what you want to hear about money. When it comes to money, it is imperative that you have selective hearing!!!

Rule # 3: Money Always Goes Where It Is Taught!

And thou shalt teach them diligently unto thy children, and shalt talk of them when thou sittest in thine house, and when thou walkest by the way, and when thou liest down, and when thou risest up. And thou shalt bind them for a sign upon thine hand, and they shall be as frontlets between thy eyes. And thou shalt write them upon the posts of thy house, and on thy gates (Deuteronomy 6:7-9).

You do not have to have a college degree in education or a teaching license to teach *The Rules To Money*. Every time you open your mouth to say anything about money, whether it is positive or negative, good or bad, you are teaching yourself and others about money. Consequently, you are such a great teacher, the lessons you have been teaching up to this point have been highly effective. You have either been teaching others the right things to say about money, or your words have been influencing others to pick up some of your own negative thinking about money.

For example, if you are constantly telling someone to turn off the lights because you are trying to save money on the electric bill, you are teaching yourself and others that there is not enough money to go around, and that you do not have the means to pay the bill. Your children, your spouse, your friends, or whatever the case might be, may not say anything to you out loud, but they would be soaking in your teachings like a sponge. They would in turn teach others what they learned without realizing it at first. Then, what they have heard would become a pattern or belief system that would be difficult for them to change. This difficulty would become evident as your loved one begins to consciously tell everyone he or she meets to turn off the lights. This person has now become a product of your teachings. And so it is with your actions!

Every action you take, and every move you make concerning money is setting precedence for others around you to follow. Let us say that you were brought up as a child to eat everything on your plate because someone around the world does not have enough food to eat, if any. Eventually, you would adopt that concept yourself. You would think it is a requirement to eat everything on your plate. If someone you knew came to your home for dinner and only ate two bites during the meal, you might become offended or agitated, if not frustrated. You would wonder what was wrong with that person.

In this case, the person in question may have been brought up to believe, or perhaps learned on his or her own, that there is plenty of food to go around in the world, as well as an abundance of everything that he or she actually needed, and that it was permissible to eat as much or as little as he or she wanted without feeling deprived or guilty.

What you have been taught about money may not be a problem at first, but if for some reason you ended up marrying someone with the opposite thought processes about money, your "paradise" might be threatened. One person is expecting the other to change his or her point of view. If the change does not take place, what then?

As a teacher, you are literally a professor, and what you actually say every time you speak about money is your profession. And like any profession, you get paid for being in that profession unless you are working strictly as a volunteer, with no pay. But in this case, every word that you speak (your profession) will either yield you a great dividend or leave you in the poor house. You are what you preach. You are what you hear. And you are what you teach. No exceptions!!!

The one thing you must know about this rule is that you are either teaching someone through your words and actions how to think abundantly or how to think poorly. Poverty thoughts only lead to lack and limitation. Rich speaking and rich thoughts will lead only to abundance.

It is important to know that the Universe is full of abundance—and is available to anyone 24 hours a day, 7 days a week, 365 days a year, 366 in leap year, without any respect of person. That is the primary lesson you must learn and believe with every fiber of your being if you are to be a teacher who thinks outside of the box.

Economically speaking, if you want to know where anyone is in their mental and scientific approach to money, just begin a conversation about the high price of gasoline. If someone says, "I cannot keep paying these ridiculous and outrageous gas prices; I will have to park my car," that person has the wrong concept of money, and will only continue to feel the pinch of what he or she perceives as a gas shortage. On the other hand, the person with the right attitude will say, "No matter how high gas prices get, I always have plenty of money to keep a full tank of gas. I have plenty of gasoline to get me anywhere I want to go!!! And that person can then spend time planning the next destination without worrying about how to get there.

For the purposes of this book, which is primarily written from a Biblically economic point of view, there is no gas shortage or any other shortage of any kind. We have been programmed to buy into that shortage mentality. The government, which is God-Ordained, may be run by humanity, but there is a higher power at work behind the scenes.

This Universe was created before any government was ever erected, and if you look carefully at the creation God created in the Book of Genesis, you will see that Adam and Eve were created by a Wealthy God to live in a Wealthy universe. Everything that Adam and Eve needed to function in this earthly habitat called the Garden of Eden was at their beck and call. Believe it or not, that world still exists if you dare to believe.

Here are some common fallacies or untruths about money that have permeated not only the world, but in the thinking processes of those who have less money than what they could have. They are the very reasons why the rich get richer and the poor get poorer:

> It is wrong to have money!
> The Love of money is the root of all evil!
> It is a sin to even think about money!
> The poor you have with you always!
> Money does not grow on trees!
> It is not God's Will for you to have money!
> Money is not Spiritual!
> Money is not Holy!
> Money cannot buy you happiness!
> I would rather have my health than money!
> In order to have money, you have to work long hours!

Here is what your reply should be to the aforementioned fallacies and untruths:

> God delights in my prosperity!
> Having money is God's idea!
> Having money is a good thing!
> As a man thinketh in his heart, so is he!
> God has brought me out into a Wealthy Place!
> I am gifted with money!
> It is God's Will for me to have money!
> Money is Holy and Spiritual!
> I am happy because I am at peace with money!
> It is okay to have health <u>and</u> wealth!
> I get paid lots of money doing what I love to do!

Every word you speak about money is teaching someone to either think correctly about money or incorrectly. Teach the wrong lesson, and that information will do more harm than good in the long run. Additionally, every thought you think, every word you speak about money, and every action you take along the lines of money is attracting into your personal space like-minded individuals who think, speak and act in the same way as you.

Why is this tidbit of information important? Speak, think, and act rich, and you will attract rich thinking, right speaking, and purposely acting persons who will add to your money mentality. As a result, you will soar financially and attract money on a scale unheard of by the world. Those who take the opposite road will only attract individuals who will find zillions of reasons to talk you out of your money before you even get started.

There is one last thought I want to leave with you concerning money. Every good teacher has to have a subject matter to teach and students to teach, therefore, a curriculum has to be in place (what is to be taught) as well as a methodology (how your subject matter will be taught).

The whole purpose of this book is to assist you in devising your curriculum and methodology. View money as your curriculum and view *The Rules To Money* as your methodology. You will have to get creative in how you will teach these rules to yourself and others. Each rule has to be understood, mastered, and constantly evaluated to determine how well you are staying on course with your money goals, especially if you have no emotional support system to keep you motivated to achieve mastery. You may be your only cheerleader, which is okay. You can get there from here if you put in the time to study your subject matter, money from every possible angle.

Rule # 4: Money Always Goes Where It Is Highly Thought Of!

Finally, brethren, whatsoever things are true, whatsoever things
are honest, whatsoever things are just, whatsoever things are pure,
whatsoever things are lovely, whatsoever things are of good report;
if there be any virtue, and if there be any praise, think on these
things (Philippians 4:8)

Someone may ask you, "How is your love life?" In such a case, they would expect for you to spill the beans on your latest romance. As a Spiritual Money Specialist, Wealth Specialist, and Money Preacher, with a Money Ministry, my first question to you might be, "How is your thought life?" Your response to this question would literally speak volumes about your wealth status.

You are what you think about all day long and all night long, even in your sleep, while you sleep. You are the total sum of every thought you think—past, present, and future. Self-talk experts suggest that we think on an average of 20,000-60,000 thoughts a day, if not more. If you are thinking the wrong thoughts about money, you can never expect to acquire astronomical wealth.

My job as a Money Preacher is to tell you those things about money that others may not tell you, simply because they think you will end up with more money than they might have. You may find this hard to believe, but money, though it is an inanimate object, has a personality, and can be offended quite easily. Knowing this particular information can work wonders for helping you to increase your cash flow by more than 1,000,000%!!! (Note: I enrolled in accounting classes just to learn how to use its principles to increase my cash flow). I had a blast in my accounting classes, by the way!!!

Have you ever been surrounded by someone who made you feel very badly, and you could not wait to get out of his or her immediate presence?

Have you ever been in a situation where the atmosphere was so negatively charged until you just had to leave as fast as you could? If the answer to that question is, "Yes," then keep reading!!!

Every single day of your life, at every second of the day and night, around the clock, you are either attracting massive wealth to you like a money magnet, or you are repelling money away from you like an insect or bug repellant—all because of what you think about money on a regular, consistent basis. For example, each time you say, "Money is hard to come by," money absolutely cannot wait to move away from you with lightning speed to go to the person's house who is thinking correctly about money and saying, "Money is easy to come by!!!" That is why the rich get richer and the poor get poorer.

The rich get wealthier with every thought. They make a conscious effort to ensure that every thought they think about money is the right thought. The rich will never think they are poor, just as someone that is poor may never be able to think they are rich—not because the poor cannot think richly; in many cases they will not. It is just not in their nature to speak richly. But, it may be in their nature to talk obsessively and incessantly about those who are rich. Such negative thinking is only wasted motion that could have been deliberately directed to thinking richly.

In today's Scripture, the challenge is to think about things that are pure, lovely, honest, and true, but to hear some people talk, you would think it was a sin to even think about money at all. If you think it is a sin to talk or think about money because you might believe that money is the root of all evil like the Bible says, why is it that many people go out of their way to say all the wrong things about money? If it is wrong to think about money, then why talk negatively about money?

When the Bible tells us that "The love of money is the root of all evil," that was a true statement, but only for those individuals who love money so much they would do the wrong thing to get that money. Would you agree that there are people out there who would kill you for a dollar, and never think twice about it, you, or your life?

If having money was wrong, why would Jesus tell Peter to go fishing for that one fish that had money in its mouth? Peter was to take that money and pay his taxes and Jesus' taxes!!! This is a classic example that Jesus wants you to have money to pay your bills with plenty of money left over to enjoy!!! Does that sound like Heaven wants you to ignore your bills because you have the wrong idea about money? I think not!!! If you pay bills, there is no way of getting around not thinking about the money that you need to pay that bill. Even the Bible is very specific about "paying your just and honest debts" ( ). Does that sound like a God who wants you to be nonchalant about money? I do not think so!!!

How much money do you want to make this year? This month? This week? This day? Or have you even thought about it? Not thinking in such a manner makes the difference between a person who makes $700 a month and a person who makes $777 Billion a month.

To keep myself on the right "money frequency" so that I could develop the right money psychology about money, I subscribed to the *Money Magazine.* I put one copy of the *Money Magazine* in every room of my house, so that no matter where I was in that room, I could see the word, "money." The principal started working immediately. The word, "money" was the first thing I saw in the morning when I woke up, and the last thing I saw before I went to sleep at night. I was impressing upon my subconscious mind all the money I wanted to have. (Incidentally, that is the very reason, I deliberately use the word, Money throughout this book. I want your subconscious mind to be so saturated with the word, Money, until you are running over in money).

I got this idea for programming my subconscious mind with money when it dawned on me that I had a Bible in every room of my house. I had visited a famous site, and I noticed that in that wealthy living space, there was not one Bible in that family's residence. It occurred to me that I could become wealthier than the people whose house I visited if they had no Bible in their house at all. They had gotten wealthy, but where was the Bible? *All these principles listed in this book are based on the Word of God. That is why I went out of my way to start each devotion with an opening Scripture.*

Did you like my *Money Magazine* idea? Can you think of more things you can do to get yourself in the habit of thinking about more and more money easily and quickly so you can begin to attract that money in less time?

Before leaving this rule to money, this would be a good time to start thinking about how much money you would love to make in one year, one month, one week, and one day if you absolutely knew there was no reason why you could not have that amount of money.

If it were possible for you to earn as much money as you wanted, guaranteed, hands down, with no questions asked, how much money would you want to earn? Write that dollar amount below. Do not be shy or stingy about the amount. Be generous with yourself!!! Have fun thinking about how much money you could actually have versus what you might be experiencing right now!!!

This is the dollar amount I want to earn in one year. _____

This is the dollar amount I want to earn in one month. _____

This is the dollar amount I want to earn in one week. _____

This is the dollar amount I want to earn in one day. _____

Rule # 5: Money Always Goes Where It Is Well Spoken Of!

So shall my word be that goeth forth out of my mouth: it shall not return unto me void, but it shall accomplish that which I please, and it shall prosper in the thing whereto I sent it (Isaiah 55:11).

It is my personal belief system that you cannot talk poor and expect to get rich, and you cannot talk rich and expect to stay broke. The problem is that poor people have difficulty talking rich, and the rich have difficulty talking poor. So, if those individuals, both poor and rich, got together in one room, they would have nothing in common to talk about.

I am an excellent listener, and I have noticed that when I talk rich, the people I am having a conversation with will develop a nonchalant attitude as if they are being highly offended by such talk. Talk to such individuals long enough and they will tell you in a straightforward, direct tone, with very little tactfulness, "I do not want to listen to that." But, when they lead the conversation themselves, they will tell you fifty reasons why they do not have the money to pay a bill.

In my opinion, individuals who talk incorrectly about money in such a fashion is nothing short of the foolish talking, jesting, and inconvenience that the Scriptures mention. Having conversations with such individuals will highly diminish, reduce, and make non-existent your own cash flow.

Talk to these individuals often enough and those persons will end up having more money than you. At some point, you have to ask yourself if this is that person's strategy to undermine your cash flow just so they can sabotage you. If that is the case, you may need to change your friends. You do not need anyone in your life that is not wishing you well.

Again, money has feelings!!! It loves to be the center of attention where everyone in the room is talking well about money. To reiterate, that is the very reason why I deliberately use the word money in virtually every sentence throughout this book. The more you say the word, "Money," the more money you will acquire. The more you say good things about your money and money in general, the more money will find its way to you with God speed (faster than the blink of an eye). "The Word of God is quick and powerful and sharper than any two edged sword" (Hebrews 4:12)!!!

In the previous rule to money, we learned that you are the total sum of all your thoughts. Again, allow me to emphasize that every single thought you think is either making you richer or poorer. And so it is with your words. Every word you speak is either bringing you one step closer to living on "easy street" or one step further away from the wealth you think you want.

Consider the following Scripture that opens today's money devotion, which just came to mind last night as I was meditating on the word, "money." Every word and thought that you think is your personal servant who will go out and bring back to you exactly what you spoke the word for.

If you sent someone to pick up groceries for you at the local market, and you had written down on a shopping list everything that you wanted, and you gave that person specific instructions to bring back everything on that list, they would bring you back everything you requested, no exceptions. Your words and thoughts work the same way.

Here are a few things I developed and put into my Wealth Portfolio to increase my money cash flow: One of which are a series of good things I wanted to say about my money:

My Money Is Abundant!

My Money Is Alive!

My Money Is Almighty!

My Money Is Amazing!

My Money Is Anointed!

My Money Is Appreciated!

My Money Is Awesome!

My Money Is Blessed!

My Money Is Big!

My Money Is Bright!

My Money Is Brilliant!

My Money Is Creative!

My Money Comes Easy!

My Money Is Compassionate!

My Money Is Clean!

My Money Came!

My Money Is Dazzling!

My Money Is Deep!

My Money Is Delightful!

My Money Is Deserved!

My Money Is Devoted To Me!

My Money Is Divine!

My Money Is Doubling!

My Money Is Enjoyable!

My Money Is Energetic!
My Money Is Exalted!
My Money Is Exciting!
My Money Is Empowering!
My Money Is Enriching!
My Money Is Fabulous!
My Money Is Fair!
My Money Is Faithful!
My Money Is Fantastic!
My Money Is Fun!
My Money Is Focused!
My Money Is Generational!
My Money Is Gifted!
My Money Is Good!
My Money Is Glorious!
My Money Is Grand!
My Money Is Great!
My Money Is Happy!
My Money Is Healthy!
My Money Is Here!
My Money Is Holy!
My Money Is Increasing!
My Money Is Infinite!
My Money Is Invigorating!
My Money Is Inside Of Me!
My Money Is Jubilee!
My Money Is Just!
My Money Keeps On Coming!
My Money Is Love!
My Money Loves Me!
My Money Is Magnetic To Me!
My Money Is Meditative!
My Money Is Multiplying!
My Money Is New!
My Money Is Omnipotent!
My Money Is Omnipresent!

My Money Is Perfect!
My Money Is Phenomenal!
My Money Is Plentiful!
My Money Is Powerful!
My Money Is Profitable!
My Money Is Prosperous!
My Money Is Pure!
My Money Is Quadrupling!
My Money Is Quantum Physics!
My Money Is Quick!
My Money Is Real!
My Money Is Relaxed!
My Money Is Respectable!
My Money Is Respected!
My Money Is Safe!
My Money Is Satisfying!
My Money Is Saved!
My Money Is Sharp!
My Money Is Spectacular!
My Money Is Splendid!
My Money Is Spiritual!
My Money Is Technical!
My Money Is Thoughtful!
My Money Is Tripling!
My Money Is Universal!
My Money Is Uncommon!
My Money Is Unlimited!
My Money Is Valuable!
My Money Is Valued!
My Money Is Welcome!
My Money Is Well!
My Money Is Wise!
My Money Is Wonderful!
My Money Is Worthy!
My Money Is Yahweh!
My Money Is Zealous!

Allow me to close today's money devotion with this Scripture found in Ephesians 5:4: "Neither filthiness, nor foolish talking, nor jesting, which are not convenient: but rather giving of thanks." Saying the wrong things about money will only keep you from reaching your highest money potential. Determine in your mind today that you will only say the right things about money. Anything less is nothing short of foolish!!!

Rule # 6: Money Always Goes Where It Can Be Afforded!

Thou hast caused men to ride over our heads; we went through fire and through water: but thou broughtest us out into a wealthy place (Psalms 66:12).

I love to develop Money and Wealth Portfolios. Years ago, I downloaded a picture of a car, a house, and a picture of a wedding couple who had just gotten married, and I incorporated these images into my portfolio. I typed these words at the bottom of the page in large, bold letters: **"No matter how much it costs, I can afford it!!!"**

A few days months ago, I added additional pictures of cruise ships, vacation homes, sports cars, expensive shopping sprees in Tokyo, Paris, and France, as well as expensive clothes, wedding gowns, and restaurants, and I typed these words at the very top of the first page: **"I Can Afford To Go Anywhere, At Any time, And Any place, To Be Anything, Have Anything, And Do Anything My Heart Desires!!! No matter how much it costs I can afford it!!!"**

Again, money has a personality and can easily be offended. Each time, and every time that you say, "I can't afford it," all the money that would have, could have, and should have stayed with you because it really wanted to, will literally exit your life to go live, dwell, abide, and reside with the person who constantly says, "I CAN afford it!!!" That is just in the one time you make such a negative statement. Who knows how much money you would lose if you keep saying what you cannot afford.

When you say "You cannot afford it [money]," money actually and literally believes you, and begins to believe that it is unaffordable. Money wants you to say that "You can afford money!!!" If you cannot afford to pay your light bill, your lights get turned off. On the same token, money is turned off by those who say "I cannot afford money!!! The more you

20

say, "I can afford it," the more turned on money gets, and the more money you will attract!!!

How many times a day do you actually say, "I cannot afford that?" How many times a day do you make a conscious effort to say, "I can afford that?" Either way, you will have what you say. Throughout this money book, the implied message is that "like attracts like." Money thinks that it can easily be afforded by its owner without any effort, therefore, money is only attracted to those with the same "like affordable" mentality.

What is the difference between a person who earns $700 a month and a person who earns $7,000,000 a month? The answer to that question is the word, "affordability." The person with the $7,000,000 mentality believes that he or she can easily afford $7,000,000. He or she does not say, "I cannot afford to have $7,000,000." They think of all the things they can and will do with that large sum of money.

On the other hand, the person with the $700 mentality must learn to say, "I can afford to have $7,000,000 a month," and maintain that "affordable thought" until he or she literally acquires that amount of money. With that said, how much money do you believe in your heart and soul that you can afford every month? Write that amount in the space provided below:

This is the amount of money I believe that I can afford each month. _____ month._____

Personally, I believe I can afford $999 Centillion (1 with 303 zeroes) every month. The higher you think, the more money you will attract. My goal in writing this book is to teach you how to think like a Centillionaire, which will ensure that you will end up with more than Millions or Billions of dollars!!!

Do not worry about how this money will come into fruition, or when. Just maintain your "affordability" financial statement: "I can afford it, whatever the cost," which reminds me of what people actually say when you ask them if they want a $1Million mansion. "Do you know how much the yearly property tax will be on a house that costs that much? You would probably have to pay $10,000 a year!!!!" Then they go on to say, "Do you think it is worth having a $1 Million mansion. Think about it!!!

What these well-meaning individuals are saying is that they would never be able to afford the $1 Million home or the $10,000 a year property tax. This is a prime example of the persons who would never have such a home. Subsequently, these are the same individuals who will try to scare you into "seeing things their way" to the point where you abandon the idea of having any kind of home of any amount.

In such cases, the money that would have come to this person to afford a $1 Million mansion and the $10,000 property tax will go to the person believing they can afford to live in a $1 Million mansion, pay the property tax, and still have more than enough left over to spend, invest, enjoy, and save.

Rule # 7: Money Always Goes Where It Is Studied!

Study to shew thyself approved unto God, a workman that needeth not to be ashamed, rightly dividing the word of truth (2 Timothy 3:16).

Doctors go to medical school to learn how to practice medicine. Attorneys go to law school to learn how to practice law. Nurses got to nursing school to learn how to practice nursing. Real Estate agents go to real estate school to learn how to practice and sell real estate. Teachers go to teaching school to learn how to practice teaching.

In keeping with this line of reasoning, it is reasonable to assume that anyone who wants to study money must go to some sort of money school to study money. This book is, if you will, your opportunity to enroll in your own personal money school to learn in the privacy of your own home how to study *The Infinite Rules To Money*, the laws of money, the personality of money, and such. Consider this book as your starting point of astronomical wealth!!!

The Infinite Rules To Money is your money curriculum. I am your Money Specialist. And this money book is your money textbook that you must study religiously day and night to master the money principles, laws, rules, and techniques outlined in this money book.

It bears mentioning here that at one time, after getting a diploma in accounting, which I only went into to master the art of increasing my cash flow by intentionally looking at Financial Statements, I decided to pursue a Bachelor's degree in Finances. I wanted to either become a financial analyst or a financial planner. One day, it dawned on me that financial planners only help their clients and customers plan the money that they already have on hand.

Financial planners cannot help you, for example, to invest billions of dollars if you do not have billions of dollars. I, on the other hand, wanted to do quite the opposite. I wanted to help individuals plan on first mentally acquiring zillions of dollars before they actually acquired that kind of money. The bottom line to money is that there is *Infinite Money* that has yet to be tapped into in this earth realm.

My money objective is for you to see that all that *Infinite Money* exists just for you, and is just waiting on you, and waiting for you, so that you can tap into it easily. Oh, if you would only believe!!! "Eye hath not seen, nor ear heard, neither has it entered into the heart of man the things which God hath prepared for them that love Him. But, they are revealed unto him [you] by the Spirit" (1 Corinthians 2:9).

I want you to feel like a Centillionaire!!! Imagine if the front cover itself contained a $1 Centillion Bill with your face on it!!! Would that be believable to you that you could attract that much money? If not, what is the most amount of money you can believe God for? You can only attract what is most believable to you!!!

Hopefully, the front cover of this book makes you feel like a Millionaire!!! Do you feel like a Millionaire looking at the image? I know I do!!! Someone once asked me what $1 Million felt like when I told them I felt like $1 Million. I simply replied, "How would you feel if you bought or purchased the car of your dreams, and were able to pay cash for it? That is how I feel like right now!!! And I am feeling richer and wealthier by the minute!!!"

And so can you if you will get that money feeling by studying the image on the front cover. You are what you look at every day!!! You are what you think about zillions of times a day!!! You are a total sum of what you say as well!!! You are what you study!!! And in this money course, you are a money student who is about to take the idea of money to Infinite Dimensions and Realms unheard of by the world!!!

One last note about Rule # 7. Everyone has heard of Millionaires, Billionaires, and Trillionaires. God wants to give you wealth that has not been heard of. Consider this information that I am absolutely delighted to share with you. These are actual figures of numbers that really exist.

one hundred, one thousand, one million, one billion, one trillion, one quadrillion, one quintillion, one sextillion, one septillion, one octillion, one nonillion, one decillion, one undecillion, one duodecilion, one tredecillion, one quattuordecillion, one quindecillion, one sexdecillion, one septendecillion, one

octodecillion, one novemdecillion, one vigintillion, and one centillion.

Most of the individuals I shared this information with had never heard of numbers past a trillion or quadrillion, let alone all the figures that I just gave you. Why is that? What would happen if the entire population of people learned how to count up to 999 Centillion? Can you imagine being a Centillionaire, or a Tredecillionaire?

For that reason, I decided to write the book, *The Little Girl Who Loved Math*, to expose everyone to these huge astronomical numbers. It is my personal belief that if you think about centillions of dollars, you will end up with a much more than $999 Million. I might add, most emphatically, that even $999 Centillion is pocket change to Almighty God whose worth is absolutely priceless!!!

But, in any respect, read all the numbers on this page that are highlighted in bold letters until you can commit them to your perfect memory bank, as well as your spiritual money bank!!! The Higher you think, the richer you will be!!!

Rule # 8: Money Always Goes To Where It Is Expected!

Cast thy bread upon the waters: for thou shalt find it after many days (Ecclesiastes 11:1).

Have you ever ordered a package of some kind that would be shipped to you by either Federal Express or UPS? In my case, I start watching for the Federal express or UPS the very next day after ordering any item.

Also, if you are to receive a letter in the mail, you deliberately set a watch on your mailbox, hoping it will arrive as quickly as possible. On the same token, if you have put in a long-work week on your job, you are expecting to get paid for the services and hours rendered.

Have you been or are you expecting money, *Infinite Money* to show up at your door step? When a pregnant woman discovers that she is expecting a child, what does she do? She will go home and start planning a nursery, pick out the baby's name, and think about how the rest of her life will be different. She will start thinking of herself as a mother, though the baby is not due for another nine months.

Are you expecting money in the same way a mother expects to give birth to her baby on its due date? What are you arranging or rearranging in your daily life to accommodate for all the money you are expecting to have? Allow me to share with you what I did to start preparing for *Infinite Money* and *Infinite Wealth*.

I started having money dreams that 7, 18-Wheelers were backing up to my front door to unload Zillions of dollars. I could see these trucks driving very slowly down my street as if they were weighed down with so much money!!! I could see the truck drivers negotiating the small, narrow road as they brought my money to me. I could see all the neighbors standing outside their homes trying to find out what the commotion was all about!!! I could see the drivers having difficulty passing one another as one truck was coming, and the other one was going to reload the truck with more money.

I could see myself mowing my lawn in the summer time so the truck driver would not have to tread down, or tread through foot-long grass just to get to my door for me to sign the money release form. I could see myself wearing comfortable clothes so that I could transport the money into my physical home. I could see what each driver was wearing. I could feel the excitement of seeing and touching all that money!!!

I also used this same technique to see myself taking briefcases of money in excess of $1Million to the bank to deposit. Every day, I made it my personal business to take millions of dollars to the bank. I was a regular depositor of millions of dollars. The bank loved me because I was depositing so much money!!! I could even see them getting special permission to give me daily Infinite Interest on every dollar I put into my multiple bank accounts just to reward me for being a faithful customer!!! The bank was paying me astronomical sums of money just to have my money in their bank!!! How wonderful!!!

I am expecting to get money from nowhere!!! I am expecting to get big money from out of the blue!!! I am expecting money—Infinite Money to come to me from the east, the west, the north, and the south!!! I am expecting money from all seven continents—yes even Antarctica!!! I am expecting to be overtaken by money from every direction, twenty-four hours a day, seven days a week.

I am expecting to be gifted with so much money, I have to spend countless hours, planning where all my funds will go to. I am expecting to have plenty of money to save, spend, enjoy, and invest. I am expecting all my money to work for me, instead of me having to waste unnecessary energy working for it, and then be too tired to even think about money!!! I am expecting money to come to me for no reason at all. My money comes to me "just because" I am expecting it!!! I am expecting my money to double, triple, and quadruple—QUICKLY!!! When it comes to money, I just have high expectancy.

I am expecting my money to do great things. My money is a great achiever who wants to reach its highest potential of multiplying. I am expecting for all my money—every single dollar to "be fruitful and multiply" according to the book of Genesis. I have high expectations of money, for money, and money will not disappoint me!!! That is why I am always getting Infinite Money because money knows that I do expect it to surpass my expectations. My money loves and aims to please!!!

Rule # 9: Money Always Goes To Where It Is Blessed!

And I will make of thee a great nation, and I will bless thee, and make thy name great; and thou shalt be a blessing: And I will bless them that bless thee, and curse him that curseth thee: and in thee shall all nations of the earth be blessed (Genesis 12:1-3).

Every time you say something good or positive about your money and money in general, you are literally blessing that money and opening up the door for more money to come. The more you bless money, the more money you will have.

Most people have no idea that they are under a money curse, a family curse, or a generational curse. You, yourself may be surrounded by one or more than one individual who may be secretly cursing you and your money so that your money will be withheld from you. Today's devotion on money is dedicated to empowering you to speak money blessings over yourself daily so that you will not be affected by these money curses.

One money blessing that you speak over yourself is more powerful than a million curses spoken against you, if you will only open your mouth and start to speak forth those money blessings, health blessings, family blessings, and generational blessings. Allow me to explain how I discovered this money principle of blessing money.

One day I was walking through my living room, and I heard these words in the spirit, in my spirit, "Someone sent a money curse to your house." I went outside and someone had deliberately left a slew of pennies at my mailbox, hoping that I would succumb to the money curse. I simply said, "Money curse, and all money curses, I bind you up in the name of Jesus."

I went on to say, "According to 1 Peter 2:24, Jesus Christ bore my money curse so I could be bound to money blessings everyday for the rest of my life. If Christ bore my money curses two thousand years ago on the cross, I do not have to bear this money curse now. In the name of Jesus, I loose my money blessings to me right now in the name of Jesus. No weapon formed against my money blessings shall prosper. All my money is under the blood of the Lamb!!!"

I began praising God that I was no longer bound to money curses. I had just preached the Gospel of Jesus Christ to myself and it worked. I enforce those money blessings daily by praying that prayer daily. I have victory over money curses, and so do you!!!

Begin to thank God for all the money you have had, have, and will continue to have!!! Thank God for all your money—past, present, and future. Whatever you bless will increase dramatically in the say way you hear about individuals who bless their crops and they end up with larger than life vegetables or whatever it was they planted.

In the Gospels, when Jesus blessed the two fishes and five barley loaves, what seemed like not enough became enough to feed over five thousand men, not counting the women and children. If that were not enough, there were twelve baskets of fragments left over.

Get in the habit of saying to every coin and bill that you have, whether it be a penny, or a $100 bill: "Bless you money, in the name of Jesus!!! Money, be blessed!!! Be fruitful and multiply Infinite fold in Jesus' name!!!" Get in the habit of saying, "Bless you money!!!" Get in the habit of saying, "I bless money!!! Pretty soon, you will have people begging you to put your hands on their money to bless it. This has happened to me quite a few times, especially by those who had previously cursed my money."

Are you willing to become a money blesser? The more you bless money, the more money you will have to bless!!! Can you dare to believe that blessing four pennies could literally lead you to have $4,000,000,000 to hold in your hands? Nothing is impossible with God, or with you, if you dare to believe, which leads to Rule # 10.

Rule # 10: Money Always Goes To Where It Is Tithed!

Will a man rob God? Yet ye have robbed me. But ye say, Wherein have we robbed thee? IN tithes and offerings. Ye are cursed with a curse: for ye have robbed me, even this whole nation. Bring ye all the tithes into the storehouse, that there may be meat in mine house, and prove me now herewith, saith the Lord of hosts, if I will not open you the windows of Heaven, and pour you out a blessing, that there shall not be room enough to receive it. And I will rebuke the devourer for your sakes, and he shall not destroy the fruits of your ground, neither shall your vine cast her fruit before the time in the field, saith the Lord of hosts. And all nations shall call you blessed: for ye shall be a delightsome land, saith the Lord of Hosts (Malachi 3:8-12).

When I wanted to increase my income to a high income status, I came up with this technique that you can easily duplicate. As a general rule, I am a tither!!! Tithing is the first Biblical principle I learned at church and took to heart immediately!!! I would actually give more than the 10% God required. On one occasion, I gave God 90% of my tithes and kept 10%.

While at church one Sunday, I took five yellow tithe envelopes and I wrote $400 on one, $4,000 on one, $40,000 on one, $400,000 on one, and $4,000,000 on the last one. I had planned later to get additional envelopes to write in the figure and the dollar amount of $4,000,000,000. I had wanted to feel what it was like to have more and more money to tithe.

I felt good knowing I had paid $400 in tithes. I felt even better when I could feel myself paying $4,000 in tithes, and I was ecstatic thinking I had 4,000,000 to tithe. Unfortunately, my pastor saw me with all the tithe envelopes stuck in my Bible, and he thought I was wasting envelopes that the church was responsible for paying for with their church funds. No one had any idea why I was using this simple spiritual technique that would not only have worked for me, but for everyone in the church if they had understood how to work this principle.

Unfortunately, the pastor's negative response threw me off guard, and I never could get back into the swing of paying any more tithes. Up to that point, I had been paying way more than a full tithe. My money flow started to dwindle. I made it up in my mind that I would only pay tithes in a place that understood the power of increase.

It just makes perfect sense that the more tithes you pay, the more money you will have to tithe. If the pastor had caught hold of this technique himself, he would have gladly given me a whole slew of tithes envelopes. $4,000,000 is more than enough money to pay for envelopes, with plenty left over for outreach programs. Do you think???

When I was fully and actively engaged in my research of trying to find out why the rich get richer and the poor get poorer, the one thing I noticed about all the famous and wealthy individuals I studied is that they all had one thing in common: they all had paid their tithes and offerings. When they were faithful in paying certain amounts initially, they would see an increase in their income, thus, they had more tithes to pay.

If they had $1, they gave God His $.10 first, before they engaged in any other transactions. When they got their first $1Million, they were faithful in paying God their $100,000.

The first 10% of all your gross income (wages earned before taxes are taken out of your paycheck) is holy and belongs exclusively to God!!! Why??? God is the Source of all your wealth. The Bible tells us in Proverbs 3: 9-10: "Honour the Lord with thy substance, and with the first fruits of all thine increase. So shall thy barns be filled with plenty, and thy presses shall burst out with new wine."

Those who pay tithes are blessed. Additionally, as mentioned in Malachi 3, the devourer—anything coming against your finances is rebuked. As mentioned in Deuteronomy 28, "blessings will overtake you!!!" And again, in Deuteronomy 8:18, you can read these words, "It is the Lord who gives you the power to get wealth." If God did not help you, you would not even have the means of making any money at all.

Let that be a lesson!!! Not everyone is tuned in to increasing their tithing flow in the way I described. Do not let that deter you from what your tithing goal is. My goal is that after giving God 90% of my tithes, I will have so much blessing on the remaining 10% that I would not even miss the 90%!!! And that will happen, quicker than I imagine!!!

The general population actually thinks that the preaching of the Scripture above is only a ploy or devise for preachers to use to "get their money." God is not trying to take money <u>away</u> from you!!! He is trying to get money <u>to</u> you. Regular tithers know two things about tithes previously mentioned: One, God is the Source of all your wealth, and the first 10% of your Gross Income is Holy and belongs to God.

Two, people who do not tithe literally brings themselves under the curse God mentioned in Deuteronomy 28 simply because God had nothing to bless. A closed fist that is so tight that you cannot get anything into it or out of it, cuts off the Blessing Flow, the Cash Flow, and the Money Flow God was trying to put into an open hand of giving. More on giving later!!!

But, in any respect, an open hand of regularly paying your tithes <u>first</u>, before you spend that money on anything else, puts one into the position of receiving regular blessings. Tithing is much more profitable than you might imagine. Consider this Tithing Chart that shows you how much you would have to pay on the following amounts of Gross Income:

$100	=	$10
$1,000	=	$100
$10,000	=	$1,000
$100,000	=	$10,000
$1,000,000	=	$100,000
$1,000,000,000	=	$100,000,000
$1,000,000,000,000	=	$$100,000,000,000

In our system of government, everyone is looking to the President and the government to assist them in some way as if whoever is in leadership is God. God allowed our American government to be put into place for a reason most people do not understand. The government is to govern and to provide leadership, but that institution of governing is not the means to an end. You must be willing to help yourself.

The wealthy, in spite of inflation, recessions, depressions, and an unstable economy, still manage to flourish financially. They are affected by the economy, as are we all, but they seem to have the kind of mentality that is "far above all principality, power, might, and dominion" (Ephesians 1:21).

After everything is said and done, either against them, or about them, the wealthy still have the wealth the rest of the population would die for!!! Why? They realize they have the power to get wealth!!! They realize they are in control of their own destiny!!! They realize that they must continue to follow *The Infinite Rules To Money* many individuals choose not to follow!!!

One last note about tithes: Following *The Infinite Rules To Money* puts you in control of your life and empowers you to help yourself. When you pay your tithes, you are better off than a person who plays the lottery religiously, hoping to win Millions of dollars. Paying tithes to God first, before you make any other transactions is a guaranteed investment that is sure to yield an unlimited return of dividends on that investment. I wonder if any of the lottery players are tithers???

Rule # 11: Money Always Goes Where It Can Be Felt!

And straightway the fountain of her blood was dried up, and she felt in her body that she was healed of that plague (Mark 5:29).

When I was a student in high school, I came home virtually every day crying because of something someone had said or done to me. My mom told me that I needed to stop wearing my feelings on my sleeve. She told me if I did not heed such advice, that I would always be crying over something.

Since that time, I have still worn my feelings on my sleeves. If I had just one penny for every time my feelings got hurt, I would be a centillionaire NOW!!!!!!!!!!! Somehow, I knew that God was going to do something to remedy or undo my crying episodes, but I had no idea until this week as to just how God would use feelings to transform my life!!!

I have often said that when changing a car tire you have to use the same jack you used to jack up the automobile to jack the car back down after the tire has been successfully changed. In my case, the feelings that used to get stepped on were going to be used to catapult me into infinite wealth!!!

The woman alluded to in today's money devotion had had female problems for twelve long years. She had went to many doctors and had spent every dime she had trying to get well. She was still sick, busted, broke, and no doubt, disgusted. But, she had heard of a man named Jesus, who was a healer. She dared to believe that Jesus would heal her.

"For she said, If I may touch but his clothes, I shall be made whole (Mark 5:28)." As soon as this woman touched the hem of Jesus' garment, she was healed instantly. According to the Scriptures, "she felt in her body that she was healed of that plague" (verse 29).

This woman was considered "unclean" because of her sickness or infirmity, and it was against the law for her to touch or be touched in any way, in public or in private. Yet, she dared to touch Jesus' garment to get what she needed. She had literally touched Jesus with her faith.

My question to you today is: Do you have the same kind of faith to believe that you, too, can be healed of any and all of your money plagues? Can you feel in your own body all the money that you want to have? If you can call forth, summon, and speak forth this kind of "money feeling," you can literally feel your way into Infinite Money!!!

Can you dare to feel the amount of money that you want to see manifested in your life? Can you feel hundred of dollars? Can you feel thousands of dollars? Can you feel millions of dollars? Can you feel billions of dollars? Can you feel trillions of dollars? Can you feel quadrillions of dollars? Can you even step out on faith and feel centillions of dollars? If you can feel all that money as you become full of the *money feeling*, you can have it? It is all in the feelings!!!

So can you see how important feelings are, and how you can use those feelings to literally feel you way into infinite wealth? Do not underestimate your feelings!!! Neither should you underestimate the feelings of all your money that is trying to get to you!!!

Money loves to be felt—before, during, and after it is received!!! So, what feelings came to mind as you read today's devotion? Did it feel impossible for you to even feel Hundreds, Thousands, Millions, Billions, Trillions, and Quadrillions of dollars? Whatever negative feelings arose may be the very hindrance that is blocking your Infinite Cash Flow and your Infinite Money Flow.

Along these lines, when I was sixteen years old, my mom had to take me to the doctor because my menstrual cycle had not yet started. The doctor either gave me a shot or some kind of medication, and my period started. Unfortunately, every month, my cycle lasted six days and my menstrual flow was heavy right up to the very last day.

Regrettably, in 2005, I was diagnosed with fibroid tumors and my cycle was once again so heavy, I used up one box of pads in one day. To remedy the situation, I had to have a hysterectomy. This example, though it may seem like it is in poor taste, is a prime example of what happens when your own Infinite Money Flow gets started. At first, working with these *Infinite Rules To Money* may lead to a small trickle of money that does not seem to be enough to drop in a bucket. Keep working with these *Infinite Rules To Money* and you could end up with more than just a trickle!!!

How would your life change for the better if you found yourself in an Infinite Money Flow—a Flow that never ended—a Flow that just kept going on and on and on like the Energizer Bunny? Would you even want that kind of Money Flow to stop once it got started? And what would all your friends and family say if they knew why such a Money Phenomenon was occurring? More importantly, can you feel that Money Flow, now????

Every day, I say, "I Feel Hundreds of dollars!!! I Feel Thousands of dollars!!! I Feel Millions of dollars!!! I Feel Billions of dollars!!! I Feel Trillions of dollars!!! I Feel Quadrillions of dollars!!!" And I allow myself to feel all that money as being mine.

And every day, I also say, "I Feel myself having more and more money!!! I Feel Wealthier than the Wealthiest!!! I Feel like I am in the top 1% of the Income Bracket!!! I can Feel myself moving from Low Income to High Income!!! I Feel myself moving from High Income to High Income faster than the speed of light and the speed of sound!!! I can Feel it!!!

Hopefully, today's devotion has inspired you to think of a myriad of ways that you can feel the amount of money that you believe that you deserve. No matter what amount you come up with, you deserve so much more!!!

Rule # 12: Money Always Goes Where It Can Be Seen!

And he answered, Fear not: for they that be with us are more than they that be with them. And Elisha prayed, and said, Lord, I pray thee, open his eyes, that he may see. And the Lord opened the eyes of the young man; and he saw; and behold, the mountain was full of horses and chariots of fire round about Elisha (2 Kings 6:16-17).

You may not realize this, but all the money you have possessed, possess, and will ever possess abides in the Spirit Realm, just waiting to be seen. Unfortunately, most individuals never step inside the Realm of the Spirit to behold Infinite Money. They, for some reason, can never see past what they can see with the physical eye.

In 1 Corinthians 2:9-10, we are given these words, "Eye hath not seen, nor ear heard, neither have entered into the heart of man, the things which God hath prepared for them that love Him. But God hath revealed them unto us by His Spirit: for the Spirit searcheth all things, yea, the deep things of God." In verse 14 of that same passage of Scripture, God goes on to say, "But the natural man receiveth not the things of the Spirit of God; for they are foolishness unto him, neither can he know them, because they are spiritually discerned."

In today's devotion, the *eye* I will be referring to is your "Spiritual Eye," and your *Mind's Eye.* This is the point where you can see into the Spirit Realm by faith with your spiritual eyes. This place has to be seen first, before all the money you want can actually be seen with the physical set of eyes you were born with. This is where most people miss it!!!

But, because you have dared pick up this book to learn how to put these *Infinite Rules To Money* into practice, you are stepping out of your comfort zone to see more and more money than you have ever seen before. Everyone, according to the Scriptures given to you on this page, cannot and will not get to this place, simply because they will refuse to see with their Spiritual Eye, what you see.

Consider the words from this additional Scripture that is found in Matthew 13:16-17. This Scripture is among my favorites. After reading it, you will see why. These words reflect your willingness to see. What are these lovely words? "But blessed are your eyes, for they see; and your ears, for they hear. For verily I say unto you, that many prophets and righteous men have desired to see those things which ye see, and have not seen them; and to hear those things which ye hear, and have not heard them."

In other words, many Millionaires, Billionaires, and Trillionaires would give anything to see the amount of money that you are seeing in your mind's eye right now!!! But according to the Scripture in 1 Corinthians 2:14, they are "Spiritually discerned!!!" Money, and all the money that you are going to have is Spiritual and so are you!!!

Can you see yourself having Hundreds of dollars? Can you see yourself having Thousands of dollars? Can you see yourself having Millions of dollars? Can you see yourself having Trillions of dollars? Can you see yourself having Centillions of dollars? The Spiritual principle mentioned here implies the following: "If you can see it, you can have it!!! This same principle worked for Abraham in the Old Testament, and they will work for you in the NOW, Right NOW!!!

"And the Lord said unto Abram, after that Lot was separated from him, Lift up now thine eyes, and look from the place where art northward, and southward, and eastward, and westward: For all the land which thou seest, to thee will I give it, and to thy seed forever. And I will make thy seed as the dust of the earth: so that if a man can number the dust of the earth, then shall thy seed also be numbered. Arise, walk through the land in the length of it and in the breath of it; for I will give it unto thee" (Genesis 13:14-17).

How can you apply these words to your own money goals? The aforementioned Scripture simply means that you can have everything you see, as far as you can see, from any direction, all at once. For practical purposes, see yourself standing up, facing straight ahead. If you were to step forward, as you keep facing straight ahead, as far as you could go, you would be stepping forward forever. Stepping forward is Infinite. You would never run out of space if you kept facing ahead, as you moved forward.

This moving forward is only in one direction. So imagine moving Northward, Eastward, Westward, and Southward as far as you can move forward, and even backwards, and diagonally. The underlined letters would then transpire into NEWS. The Good News, which is what this *Infinite Rules To Money* is, actually demonstrates all the money you can see from all directions. There is no limit to how much money you can see with your Spiritual Eye!!! If you dare to see all that Infinite Money in the Spiritual and in the Supernatural, you can convert it all into the Physical Realm where you can see it with your Physical Eye.

Millionaires and Billionaires who live in luxury often mention the square footage of their dwelling place. For example, the square footage of a home may be 159 X 200. This information would be important to anyone wanting to know how large a home is before purchasing it. You Infinite Money works the same way. *As Far As You Can See Money, In Any Direction,* is your Infinite Money. It exemplifies the square footage of all your Infinite Money!!!

The point I am trying to make is that you can increase the square footage of your money by literally forcing yourself to see more and more money. Just as there is no limit to how much money you can see in your Mind's Eye, with your Mind's Eye, there is no limit to how much money you can have. I have never heard one Millionaire or Billionaire say, "I have so much money now, I do not need one more dollar. And you will never hear anyone say that. But, on the other hand, you may have some individuals who cannot see themselves having one more dollar!!!

Can you see yourself getting raises and promotions? Can you see yourself moving from $700 a month to $7,000,000,000 a month? Can you see yourself enjoying all the money you see yourself with? Again, if you could not see yourself moving from $700 a month to $7,000,000,000 a month, once you take care of why you feel you could never have that amount of money, you can attract any amount quickly!!!

Rule # 13: Money Always Goes Where It Can Be Had!

And the disciples came, and said unto Him, Why speakest thou unto them in parables? He answered and said unto them, Because it is given unto to know the mysteries of the Kingdom of Heaven, but to them it is not given. For whosoever hath, to him shall be given, and he shall have more abundance: but whosoever hath not, from him shall be taken away even that he hath (Matthew 13:10-12).

This rule is the main reason that prompted me to continue typing this manuscript against all odds so that it could be published quickly. The number one thing that people say when talking about their money is "I do not have any money!!! I do not have money!!! And I am not going to say I have money if I do not have it. That would be lying. You cannot get blood from a turnip!!!!!!" Then, such individuals will give you twenty-five zillion reasons why money is not important anyway!!!

Nothing could be further and farther from the truth. But, in my case, I asked God to tell me how it was possible to get money when you literally and actually do not have it. When I first read this Scripture years ago, I did not have any money at all, but I knew that all the money that I wanted and desired were all in the Spiritual Realm. What God said to me that day shocked me beyond words!!!

God simply said, "People who have large sums of money have followed all *The Infinite Rules To Money* that you are just learning about. That is why more and more money keeps coming to them. In your case, the only way to acquire money that you do not have, or think you do not have, is to trick your subconscious mind into thinking you have lots and lots of money." You will have to learn how to transfer all the *Infinite Money* that you have in your Heavenly, Spiritual Bank Account, into your physical bank accounts."

I do not confess to thoughts of fear, but Matthew 13 scared me beyond words. It made me think that I would lose the hope of acquiring massive and Infinite Money before I could even have it in my physical hands. Also, at that moment, I did not think this principle was fair to anyone who did not have money. So I did what God said!!!! I found a way to trick my subconscious mind into thinking I had avalanches of money!!! And it worked!!!

First, I had taught myself to say, "I have plenty of time," when I felt test anxiety, and I lost the anxiety. I thought I would be successful in saying, "I have plenty of money!!!" And it worked!!! In fact, using this principle worked so well, I started attracting individuals who started hating me because I was having more and more money. As a result of being surrounded by these individuals, the money I was acquiring rapidly started to dwindle and taper off.

By the way, these were the individuals who would never take time to work these principles, though they were breaking *The Infinite Rules To Money* every time they opened their mouths to tell me a myriad of reasons why thinking about money in such a capacity was wrong and evil.

Some of us cannot even fathom having *Infinite Money* in a physical bank account, whereas the wealthiest of the wealthy can see themselves having multiple Swiss Bank Accounts. My question to you is how much money can you see yourself having? Can you see yourself having Hundreds of dollars? Can you see yourself having Thousands of dollars? Can you see yourself having Millions of dollars? Can you see yourself having Billions of dollars? Can you see yourself having Trillions of dollars? Can you see yourself having more than a Trillion dollars?

According to The Infinite, which is God, there is no limit to how much money you can have at any one time!!! If God were to walk up to you personally and tell you that He was going to give you all the money you could possibly want, if you simply gave him the dollar amount you absolutely wanted, how much money would you ask God For?

This is not one of those times for you to be modest about how much money you would want to have!!! This is not the time to ask God for just enough to either "get by," or just enough to pay your bills!!! According to Ephesians 3:20, "God is able to do exceeding abundantly above all that you can ask or think!"

If you think you only want a $1,000,000 and ask God for that amount, He is quite rich enough to give you more than that!!! In fact, asking God for less than what He wants to give you is an insult to Him!!! Why? You put God in a box!!! You are literally saying to God that He is not capable of being a great Heavenly Father to you?

No parent in their right mind would give their children everything they want when they want it. Otherwise, the child would become spoiled and ungrateful, and would only hit you up for more and more "stuff" later. But, here, is it plausible to think that God would live in Heaven, with all that *riches in glory* (Philippians 4:19) and allow his dearly beloved children to live in less than His best?

So many individuals are living way beneath their privilege simply because they do not take the time to look in the Bible, the Infallible, Incorruptible Word of God to see what God says they have. What good would it do if you had an inheritance of $555,555,555 that you knew or did not knew you had? Would you not agree that having $555,555,555 would change your life?

The bottom line is that you are absolutely PRICELE$$ to God and that PRICELE$$NE$$ means that you are richer than you thought!!! Can you see yourself having more and more money? Can you see yourself living the "good life" because you have all that money???? If you cannot see yourself having "all that wealth," you can be absolutely sure that you will not attract *Infinite Money.*

A final word about **Rule # 13: Money Always Goes Where It Can Be Had!!!** Money thoroughly enjoys being had—over and over and over again!!! It especially loves to go to those who desire to have more and more money? The more money you want to have, the more money you will attract quickly and effortlessly.

Rule # 14: Money Always Goes To Where It Is Written!

But He answered and said, It is written, Man shall not live by bread alone, but by every word that proceedeth out of the mouth of God (Matthew 4:4).

In this particular passage of Scripture, Jesus had been in the wilderness for forty day and forty nights. He had been fasting during that time, with nothing to eat. Satan came and presented Jesus with three different temptations—all of which satan was hoping that Jesus was fail.

To make a long story short, Jesus passed each temptation with flying colors. How did Jesus pass these temptations? He said three times these words, which are the foundation of today's money devotion: "It is written."

As a Bible Scholar, you will discover that both God and Jesus love to write. In the Old Testament, God wrote on tables of stone with his very own finger the Ten Commandments. In the New Testament, specifically in one of the Books of the Gospel, a woman was caught in the very act of adultery and the men of the town brought her before Jesus so she could be condemned for her sins.

As Jesus stooped on the ground, writing whatever it was that he was writing, one by one, the men, from the oldest to the youngest left the woman behind as they quickly exited the scene. When Jesus asked the woman where were her accusers, she merely said, "there is no man, Lord left to condemn me." Jesus told her to go in peace and that He was not condemning her either. What was it that Jesus wrote on the ground that caused the men to abandon their condemnation of the woman openly and publicly? Had He written down their own sins?

This illustration was given to emphasize the power of the written word!!! You are what you see, you are what you hear, you are what you preach, you are what you teach, and you are what you write. The question

I have for you today is, what will you choose to write about your money and your financial lot in life?

A couple of days ago, I lost my glasses and could not find them for about a week. One of the places I looked for my glasses was in the glove compartment of my car. I knew they were not there, but I was desperate to find my glasses. I did not need them to read, but I did need them to drive and to watch television. I did find, however, the four yellow tithing envelopes I mentioned to you when we were discussing the topic of tithing.

Again, I had written down on each envelope a specific amount of money. The greatest amount that I wrote down was $4,000,000. I wanted to know what it would feel like if I had $4,000,000 to tithe. If I had in fact tithed a total of $4,000,000, that would mean I had earned $40,000,000 along the way during that pay period. Of course, I felt great thinking about money in such a magnificent manner!!!

This example reminded me of another writing technique I used to attract more and more money into my life. For two consecutive years in a row, I worked as a tax preparer for an income tax office. I do not have to tell you how much I loved this job. I do not know what I liked more— looking at all the large checks I handed out to the customers every day, or keying in by computer the gross income for each customer.

I immensely enjoyed seeing how much money each person had earned during the tax year!!! Based on that information, I could process in my mind whether each family was a low income or high income family. I wondered how I could move my income to the highest income bracket in the shortest amount of time.

Additionally, I did not stop there. During our in-class training of filling out practice tax forms both electronically and on the tax forms itself, I got this grandiose idea of pretending that I had earned $4,000,000 during the tax season. I filled out my own tax form as if I had actually earned that amount of money. Once I filled out the form, I incorporated that tax document into my portfolio. Every day, I would look at my tax return and believe that I could earn that amount of money, not just in a year, but in one month or one week.

As you might know, the subconscious mind does not know whether anything is true or false. It will only act upon whatever program you give it!!! When I completed my tax form, my subconscious mind did not know whether I had actually earned that much money or not. Nor was it going to argue with me and tell me twenty-five zillion reasons why someone like me could not make $4,000,000 in one day, one week, one month, or one year.

You literally become what you write or write down!!! That is why we are told in Habakkak 2: 2-3: "And the Lord answered me, and said, Write the vision and make it plain upon tables, that he may run that readeth it. For the vision is yet for an appointed time, but at the end it shall speak, and not lie: though it tarry, wait for it; because it will surely come, it will not tarry."

This passage implies that whatever you wrote down would surely come to pass. Would that thought not inspire you to write down Hundreds, Thousands, Millions, Billions, Trillions, and Quadrillions of dollars? If you knew you would receive whatever amount of money you deliberately wrote down, would you not take the time to write down the largest amount of money known to man?

That was the very reason I deliberately wrote the Manuscript: *The Little Girl Who Loved Math* and e-mailed it to publishing consultant at Trafford Publishing!!! I had received information from a local junior college concerning all the numbers that immediately follows the number, trillion. I wondered why most of the population had gone through the public school system or the private sector without hearing about such exponential numbers.

So, you can see why I integrated these words into the manuscript I sent to Trafford Publishing:

As early as Kindergarten, Mathematicia was easily counting her numbers from one to centillion while her classmates were only counting up to one hundred. During recess, as Mathematicia jumped rope on the playground, she would be overheard counting: "one centillion one, one centillion two!!!"

When her teacher, Mrs. Hernandez, asked Prudence other ways she knew how to count, she gleefully regurgitated these words: "one hundred, one thousand, one million, one billion, one trillion, one quadrillion, one quintillion, one sextillion, one septillion, one octillion, one nonillion, one decillion, one undecillion, one duodecilion, one tredecillion, one quattuordecillion, one quindecillion, one sexdecillion, one septendecillion, one octodecillion, one novemdecillion, one vigintillion, and one centillion (1 with 303 zeroes)."

Mathematicia continued to count: "999 centillion, 999 vigintillion, 999 novemdecillion, 999 octodecillion, 999 septendecillion, 999 sexdecillion, 999 quindecillion, 999 quattuordecillion, 999 tredecillion, 999 duodecillion, 999 undecillion, 999 decillion, 999 nonillion, 999 octillion, 999 septillion, 999 sextillion, 999 quintillion, 999 quadrillion, 999 trillion, 999 billion, 999 million, 999 thousand, 999."

It is my personal theory that the higher you count, the more money you will attract into your life. Familiarize yourself with the aforesaid words and numbers. We will see them again when we discuss additional rules. At this point, I am trying to be redundant in reiterating these high numbers over and over like clockwork until they are absorbed into your subconscious mind.

Might I add that I had no choice but to write the Manuscript, *The Little Girl Who Loved Math,* because children would have no problem at all reciting these large numbers. Consider these numeric figures to be your *Language of Money!!!!!!*

Years ago, my mom said something to me that I will never forget!!! She said she heard a man on television say that Americans think too small. If no one that I know has heard of the number, centillion, I would concur with what my mom said.

In elementary school, our class was always "writing off" (start with the number 1,000, subtract the number 2, write down the sum, subtract 1, and continue with the process until you got to 0). If this process was utilized by our teacher to maximize positive reinforcement, why can this process not work for those who greatly desire to attract *Infinite Money?*

Why, then, could adults such as yourself not take the time to memorize and write down "your numbers" from Zero to Centillion? Will you dare memorize these numbers? Will you dare practice reading these numbers aloud to impress upon your subconscious mind all that wealth?

Personally, when I first learned that these numbers beyond Trillion existed, I felt cheated by my whole academic experience. I have been in school long enough to have a Ph.D., yet, I had never heard of such numbers. I had heard the number Zillion being thrown around, but in reality, there is no such number as a Zillion. It is just a slang word that everyone picked up.

But, why have those numbers not being taught to students. At least throw these numbers around in your head a couple of times before deciding whether or not you want them as part of your daily experience!!! But, in any case, you are what you write!!!

Rule # 15: Money Always Goes To Where It Is Wanted!

The young lions do lack, and suffer hunger: but they that seek the Lord shall not want any good thing (Psalms 34:10).

Originally, I had not intended to include today's rule in this book. I simply had not thought of it. However, after I had started typing this manuscript, it dawned on me how powerful this rule actually is, if it is applied with the same spirit that I have seen this rule work when men utilize it to charm a lady.

Next to the name of Jesus, I personally believe that the two most powerful statements on the face of the earth are: "I want you!!!" and "I want!!!" By nature, I am both a psychologist and scientist at heart. My favorite pastime is to ask questions and set up unsuspecting scientific experiments that either prove, refute, or disprove a hypothesis that I created in my mind. One of the things I find most fascinating is how effective the words, "I want" and "I want you!!!" are when men employ them.

Of course, let me go record by saying that I am 100% female, yet I have never seen one woman using the technique I am about to mention. Perhaps, this is just a strategy that works best for men. I grew up in a house with a father, who once he had made up in his mind that he wanted to buy or purchase a new car or truck did so, regardless of whether my mom thought he should go ahead with this kind of transaction or not.

My dad also wanted to purchase a double-wide trailer. He did in fact end up with such a home for himself. Unfortunately, he only did so after he and my mom divorced. My mom and dad may have split up, but ultimately my father got the double-wide trailer he wanted!

Along those lines, I have also noticed that once a man sets his sights on a particular female, he will stop at nothing until he gets what he wants, even if it takes a year or more. And all the man has to do is simply say, "I want you," or "I want." These two statements are used with such frequency, persistence, relentlessness, and velocity, the men in fact do seem to "divide and conquer," and the woman never sees it coming.

Then, I started to think that if men had a penny for every time they said, "I want you!!!!" to a woman, they would be Multi-Centillionaires by now. Men just seem to have a knack for getting whatever they want, simply because they want it!!!"

Money, whether you believe it or not, works in exactly the same compelling way! What would happen, exactly, if a man walked up to money in the same way he might approach a female and said, "I want you $100's (Hundreds) of dollars? I want you $1,000's (Thousands) of dollars? I want you $1,000,000's (Millions) of dollars!!! I want you $1,000,000,000's (Billions) of dollars!!! I want you $1,000,000,000,000's (Trillions) of dollars!!! Money would virtually be compelled to give in to such a compelling desire to be with the man, whether it wanted to or not, just like a female who may insist for over a year that she wants to wait for the wedding night!!!

Today's rule to money may not be as tasteful as one might expect, but, nonetheless, there is nothing like the power of want!!! It dawned on me that if these techniques work for a man who wants what he wants, when he wants it, the way he wants it, you and I can use these same techniques to want money in the same way.

I literally started saying, and I continue to say every day, "I want you Hundreds of dollars!!! I want you Thousands of dollars!!! I want you Millions of dollars!!! I want you Billions of dollars!!! I want you Trillions of dollars!!! I want you Quadrillions of dollars!!! I want you Centillions of dollar!!! I want you today, right now!!! No matter how long it takes, I will have you money, whenever I want you, however, I want you, wherever I want you, and I know you want me, too!!!

You can have as much money as you want, whenever you want it, the way you want it, if you dare to believe!!! Will you dare to adopt this principle as your own with respect to money? In my mind, this particular *Infinite Rule To Money* seems to have the kind of effect that none of the other rules have, though I guarantee they all are powerful when you apply them. However, there seems to be some compelling, force of nature behind today's rule that I cannot even begin to explain, simply because I am not a male. Yet, I am a living witness that this rule is most effective when men apply this rule to sexual intimacy and to any other thing they think they want.

But, I am sure you have heard that adage, "If it is not broke, do not fix it." Because I have seen firsthand that this rule works when men set out to be as charming as Casanova, I would be a fool not to apply this same methodology to my own money goals. People stick to what actually works!!!

Rule # 16: Money Always Goes To Where It Is Read!

Blessed is he that readeth, and they that hear the words of this prophecy, and keep those things which are written therein: for the time is at hand (Revelation 1:3).

This manuscript has been sitting on hold for at least two years, as I contemplated publishing it, simply because most people got offensive or downright nasty when I mentioned the word, money, to them. Listening to many of these individuals' disdain in talking about money correctly discouraged me to the point where I almost decided never to publish the book at all.

I changed my mind, however, when I realized that I had no choice but to go ahead with the book. Far too many individuals were breaking *The Infinite Rules To Money*, both consciously and unconsciously, and I felt that I had to continue typing this manuscript just to validate to myself that the rules had in fact worked for me, and will continue to work if I continue to employ them.

Before going any further, allow me to share with you what today's Bible Scripture in Revelation 1: 3 says in the Amplified Bible!!! I think it highly lends itself to the point I wish to make. "Blessed (happy, to be envied) is the man who reads aloud [in the assemblies] the word of this prophecy: and blessed (happy, to be envied) are those who hear [it read] and who keep themselves true to the things that which are written in it [heeding them and laying them to heart], for the time [for them to be fulfilled] is near."

As I daily typed the words to this manuscript, something inside of me was responding to each and every word I was literally reading as I went along with this project. It dawned on me that at the age of five (the time I started Kindergarten), I was already reading beyond a 6th Grade level. I was to the reading world what Mozart and Beethoven were, and still are, to the music world. I realized that being gifted to read at such an early age was no accident. I was born to read my way into *Infinite Money* and *Infinite Wealth* that the world has never heard of.

I have spent the last ten years researching everything concerning money and wealth. I had to decipher what was true, what was hype, and what was nothing more than someone's get rich quick scheme to get rich at someone else's and everyone else's expense. During this time, I read every piece of information I could find.

I bought as many books on wealth and money that I could get my hands on. I read every single word in the Bible, God's Infallible and Incorruptible Word, to uncover the mysteries of Biblical Economics. I absorbed all the wealth of data I located like a sponge, dispelling and discarding anything that was not useful to my mode of thought.

One of my main complaints in being a Money Preacher, Money Teacher, and A Wealth Specialist, with a Money Ministry is that it gets lonely at the top, with no one to talk to except God about what He actually thinks about the Wealth System, and the Laws of the Universe He set up to ensure that everyone has access to *Infinite Wealth* and *Infinite Money*.

I had started having conversations with myself just to keep following *The Infinite Rules To Money*. No one wanted to talk about having lots and lots of money. No one wanted to talk about what they would do if they had Millions and Billions of dollars. Yet, these individuals still insisted on talking about lack, limitation, and money shortages, not to mention how it was the government's fault that they could not seem to forge ahead financially.

I got an opportunity to go to Los Angeles, California to attend a weekend meeting that would teach the 150 invited attendees how to give a two-minute spill to a movie producer as to why they might want to turn your book into a movie deal. I elected not to go to Los Angeles for family reasons, but I was still disappointed that I could not go.

But, in my disappointment, I realized that I had a Divine Appointment with destiny. One day, I would go to California, but a much greater door was emerging, now! Once, I thought that I would have to move to a place in the United States where it was the norm to talk about Millions, Billions, and yes, even Trillions of dollars without feeling like you are out of place. But, then, I discovered God's plan for my reading gift.

It never occurred to me until yesterday what one of my ultimate money goals was. It could not have come at a better time. As I was meditating daily on the words I typed on each single page of this book, on each specific rule, and on the word, money, itself when everyone wanted me to view the word, money, as if it were some sort of dirty word, I realized that there was a way to keep reading my way into *Infinite Money.*

It came to me that I could start my quest for doing a more in depth study of the world's richest people on the planet. So, I went to the following Website: http://www.forbes.com/billionaires/list/ to read the Forbe's Article on *The World's Wealthiest Billionaires.* I was excited beyond words. I now had access to Billionaires. Somehow, they would become my guides to uncovering the secrets of acquiring *Infinite Money.* I would read about every person on the list and allow that *Money Feeling* to overtake me.

As I read the names of each Billionaire on the list, and where they ranked on the numbers chart, it dawned on me that I, too, was going to be on the list as being the richest Billionaire in the world. I would have more than $69 Billion. I knew reading would get me there.

Money Always Goes To Where It Is Read!!! If you want wealth, if you want *Infinite Money,* you must read the autobiographies, biographies, and even the unauthorized biographies of the richest of the rich. In short, I downloaded this list to my flash drive, and one by one, I started to read about the people on the list. I read every word of every book and every print out until I could feel all that wealth and money being generated into my own *Money and Wealth Consciousness.*

Oddly enough, I started feeling wealthier and richer than the richest individuals on the planet. I believed I could surpass them!!! And then, Christ said to me these words coming from 2 Corinthians 5:17: "Therefore, if any man be in Christ, he is a new creature: old things are past away, and behold, all things are become new." What was the interpretation: "If you Live In Christ, Dwell In Christ, Reside In Christ, and Abide In Christ, you are richer than anyone you choose to read about.

Right now, at this very moment, Friday, April 13 2012, I begin typing today's devotion where I left off yesterday. However, earlier this morning at 10 a.m. I went to the Website given to you above and downloaded thirteen pages of the top 100 Billionaires in the world. This weekend, my own personal homework assignment is to read this list day and night until I absorb all the wealth. My goal is to be on the same list, and I plan to have more than $69 Billion.

I am an author and short story novelist, and I deliberately write about money topics that I can easily go back and read later that will impress my subconscious mind with large sums of money. For example, I am currently in the process of typing another manuscript, *The Reading Specialist*, to emphasize the importance of how you can read your way into that which you want to acquire—whether it be health or wealth.

You are what you read. Again, that is why we were told to in Joshua 1:8 to "meditate in the book of the law day and night that we might observe to do according to all that is written therein." Why? Then, and only then, "will you make your way prosperous, and then you will have good success." You cannot and will not have success unless you meditate on, meditate in, read, and speak forth that which you want to create.

Today, I challenge you to go to the following Website that I gave you so that you can start to read about *Infinite Money*: http://www.forbes.com/billionaires/list/. Study the list of individuals that are on the *Money List*. Can you see yourself being one of these Billionaires? Can you see yourself being at the top of the list, or in the top 100, or even in the top 400?

At this point, I highly suggest that you acquire a wealthy looking journal that makes you feel absolutely wealthy, and write down any thoughts, feelings, and emotions you felt as you read about the people that are on the list. For that matter, also write down all the emotions, thoughts, and opinions you have as you have read this book thus far. These insights will give you invaluable information on your own thoughts and perceptions about money. Have fun in the process!!!

Rule # 17: Money Always Goes To Where It Is Welcome!

And the Spirit and the bride say, Come. And let him that heareth
say, Come. And let him that is athirst come. And whosoever will,
let him take the water of life freely (Revelation 22: 17).

No one loves to stay in a place where he or she is not welcome. Money is no exception. In today's money devotion, imagine that you have just been appointed by the President of the United States to serve your country as either the Secretary of Money and/or the Ambassador of Money. In your newly-elected position, it is your sole responsibility to welcome into your country all the money that is to be coming from the north, the east, the west, and the south.

My question to you is, how much money will you be planning on welcoming? Can you see yourself welcoming Hundreds, Thousands, Millions, Billions, Trillions, Quadrillions, and even Ccentillions of dollars? What will you do to welcome all this money? What will you do to make all that expected money feel welcome? What will you have to rearrange on your schedule or in your immediate space where the money is expected to come to, just to accommodate all that money? Will you even have enough space to house all that money that is coming in on your watch?

What else will you do to make room for Hundreds, Thousands, Millions, Billions, Trillions, and Centillions of dollars? What will be on your planned *Money Itinerary?* Will you have some sort of money celebration, a money parade, a money party, or a special dinner? Will you get dressed up? Will you buy a new wardrobe of clothes? Will you buy a new car or a new truck, or even a new house?

Better yet, what do you plan to do with all that money? Note: Be very specific and definite about the amount of money you will be welcoming!!! Only you can decide how much money you will actually be welcoming!!!

It is often customary for domestic or foreign diplomats to take their invited guests on a guided tour of the city. Where will you be taking all your money?

Again, money loves to feel welcome, and if it feels welcome, once it leaves your presence, it will go out and tell *like money* about the great time it had in your presence. It will encourage more money of like quantities, and all other interested money who wants to come along for the ride, to seek out a personal invitation so it to, can feel *extra welcome!!!*

For practical purposes, money thinks of itself as a *Very Important Person* (V.I.P.) that is just as much royalty as a King, Queen, Duke, Duchess, Prince, or Princess. It expects extra special care, extra special attention, extra tender loving care, and every other bonus that you might extend.

Money also thinks it is a daddy's girl. By that, I mean that all the money that wants to feel welcome by you has this crazy idea that you will go all out for it and that you will spare no expense to make it feel welcome. There is nothing more miserable than being in the presence of someone who constantly complains about lack, poverty, limitation, and shortage.

Your money does not like to hear about how bad you have it due to the state of the economy. Remember, these *Infinite Rules To Money* are Spiritual Laws, and in the Spirit Realm—in the Realm where God lives—*Infinite Money* lives in God's Economy, "far above all principality, power, might, and dominion" (Ephesians 1:21). That is why money would love to hear about the Billionaires that are in the top 100 of the Billionaire's list. Money wants to be in an environment where its productivity and multiplicity potential can become Infinitely Exponential!!!

Lastly, what will you wear during your reign as Ambassador of Money and/or Secretary of Money? Can you see your banner? What color is it? Can you see yourself purchasing new clothes to match your *Money Mentality, Money Psychology, and Money Consciousness?* Can you see everything concerning your pageantry, majesty, and reign in explicit detail, from start to finish?

Will or will all that money feel welcome by you? After everything is said and done, will you, your money, and all that *Incoming Money* walk away from such a festivity feeling wealthier than when you first started? Can you see your next opportunity to welcome even more money, once money puts the word out about how welcome it felt.

Hundreds of dollars will go out and attract other hundreds of dollars. Thousands of dollars will go out and talk other Thousands of dollars into coming into your immediate space. Millions will also go out and do the same, and likewise for Billions, Trillions, and Centillions. Can you handle all that money? Now is the time to prepare for it, so you will not be surprised in how much money you will have to welcome!!!

Rule # 18: Money Always Goes To Where It Is Counted!

For which one of you, intending to build a tower, sitteth not down first, and counteth the cost, whether he have sufficient to finish it? Lest happily, after he hath laid the foundation, and is not able to finish it, all that behold it began to mock him, saying, this man began to build, and was not able to finish (Luke 14:29-30).

Allow me to recall an excerpt of words I mentioned in a previous rule: So, you can see why I integrated these words into the manuscript I sent to Trafford Publishing:

As early as Kindergarten, Mathematicia was easily counting her numbers from one to centillion while her classmates were only counting up to one hundred. During recess, as Mathematicia jumped rope on the playground, she would be overheard counting: "one centillion one, one centillion two!!!"

When her teacher, Mrs. Hernandez, asked Prudence other ways she knew how to count, she gleefully regurgitated these words: "one hundred, one thousand, one million, one billion, one trillion, one quadrillion, one quintillion, one sextillion, one septillion, one octillion, one nonillion, one decillion, one undecillion, one duodecilion, one tredecillion, one quattuordecillion, one quindecillion, one sexdecillion, one septendecillion, one octodecillion, one novemdecillion, one vigintillion, and one centillion (1 with 303 zeroes)."

Mathematicia continued to count: "999 centillion, 999 vigintillion, 999 novemdecillion, 999 octodecillion, 999 septendecillion, 999 sexdecillion, 999 quindecillion, 999 quattuordecillion, 999 tredecillion, 999 duodecillion, 999 undecillion, 999 decillion, 999 nonillion, 999 octillion, 999 septillion, 999 sextillion, 999 quintillion, 999 quadrillion, 999 trillion, 999 billion, 999 million, 999 thousand, 999."

It is my personal theory that the higher you count, the more money you will attract into your life. Familiarize yourself with the aforesaid words and numbers. We will see them again when we discuss additional rules. At this point, I am trying to be redundant in reiterating these high numbers over and over like clockwork until they are absorbed into your subconscious mind.

Might I add that I had no choice but to write the Manuscript, The Little Girl Who Loved Math, because children would have no problem at all reciting these large numbers. Consider these numeric figures to be your Language of Money!!!!!!

Most individuals whom I shared the aforementioned manuscript with had difficulty in believing that the main character in that story, a mere five year old, could count numbers with such phenomenal ease. Likewise, when I also shared a manuscript of *The Luckiest Girl In Luckyville,* whose main character, also a five year old, ended up opening up a money-market account at the Luckyville Bank for $450,000—money she earned by selling lemonade at a farmer's market during the summer, everyone freaked out. They just could not believe that a five—year old could end up with all that wealth.

Children believe in the impossible, against all odds, simply because that is what children do. In these two books, which will be published soon, I deliberately used these five—years old to prove the point that these *Infinite Rules To Money* are so easy a child could implement them with phenomenal success before someone your age and mine would get started!!! Why is that?

Neither of the two main characters in my books, as a five year old, had any problems talking correctly about money or counting as high as they could possibly go. It was a game they loved to play over and over because they had every confidence in the world that they could win *in the Money Game*!!! None of the people I talked to had any clue that there was such a number as Centillion.

In fact, just saying the number, Centillion, sparked outbursts of laughter that came straight from the belly. Once this laughter started, the persons in the process of laughing could not stop.

The only reply I can think of at the moment is this: Keep following *The Infinite Rules To Money* with so much faithfulness and diligence until you find yourself laughing all the way to the bank to deposit more than $450,000!!! You will have the last laugh because you know the *Infinite Rules To Money* actually work!!!

Like Mathematicia, will you dare count: "one centillion one, one centillion two!!!" Will you dare count: "one hundred, one thousand, one million, one billion, one trillion, one quadrillion, one quintillion, one sextillion, one septillion, one octillion, one nonillion, one decillion, one undecillion, one duodecilion, one tredecillion, one quattuordecillion, one quindecillion, one sexdecillion, one septendecillion, one octodecillion, one novemdecillion, one vigintillion, and one centillion.

Will you dare count: "999 centillion, 999 vigintillion, 999 novemdecillion, 999 octodecillion, 999 septendecillion, 999 sexdecillion, 999 quindecillion, 999 quattuordecillion, 999 tredecillion, 999 duodecillion, 999 undecillion, 999 decillion, 999 nonillion, 999 octillion, 999 septillion, 999 sextillion, 999 quintillion, 999 quadrillion, 999 trillion, 999 billion, 999 million, 999 thousand, 999."

Will you dare humble yourself as a child and say these numbers out loud, every day and every night, without fail, "just because?" Will you even take the time to google these numbers to see how many zeroes each of these numbers have in front of them, just to impress your subconscious mind with all that money? Or will you just laugh away your fortune?

Laugh in the face of money and it will go elsewhere to where people are literally counting on counting all those numbers. Even now, I wonder if the richest person in the world has heard of the number Centillion. Would they even dare believe they can have more than a $1,000,000,000 (Billion)? If they have not heard, why not? And if so, are the richest people in the world counting on being at least a Quadrillionaire, or is that too much to ask?

According to Ephesians 3:20, "God is able to do exceeding abundantly above all that you can ask or think," which means that God wants to give you more than a Billion dollars, just to raise up everybody's *Money Consciousness* as well as their *Wealth Consciousness.*"

Also in 1 Corinthians 2:9, The Apostle Paul said, "Eye hath not seen, nor ear heard, neither have entered into the heart of man the things that God has prepared for them that love Him. But they are revealed unto him by the Spirit." God is using me right now to tell you that God wants to give you the kind of money that no one has heard about.

Everyone has heard of Hundreds of dollars!!! Everyone has heard of Thousands of dollars!!! Everyone has heard about Millions of dollars!!! Everyone has heard of Trillions of dollars!!! But no one I know, or talked to, has heard about Quadrillions or Centillions of dollars. I assume that there are people in the world who have heard about these numbers such as Centillion. But, in that case, why have you not heard it, until now? Why did anyone who knew not tell the general population?

Personally, I believe that if everyone in the world—whether it be in the richest country or in the poorest—were taught how to count and regurgitate all these numbers in the same way we are taught to conjugate a verb or recite our "time tables" each of them would be in a higher status than a Billionaire. Perhaps someone does not want others to know simply for that reason.

The bottom line is that once you start thinking correctly about money, and develop a money consciousness that is second to none, no government, no system, no political party, no friend, or no enemy could keep you out of that wealth. Perhaps that is why God wanted me to write this book, against all the odds. He must have wanted you to get about your business of programming your mind to receive all that money.

For that reason, I have stepped out in faith and literally bombarded your Spirit with the word, money, when others dare to tell you that thinking about, talking about, speaking about, reading about, and writing about, and following the *Infinite Rules To Money* is nothing short of treason. You may have already broken *The Infinite Rules To Money*, out of a lack of knowledge about what people actually think about the word, money.

But, today is a new day. You must rise above all forms of negativity about money so that you can acquire it. When thirsty person gets so thirsty, he or she will attempt to do something about quenching that thirst, the thirst will no longer be a problem. When you become as desperate as I did when I was employed for four years, you will find a solution.

My solution was to search money and wealth out diligently through my own independent research. What I found was better than I expected!!! I discovered the *Infinite Rules To Money* that others may have known about, but did not speak, because they thought someone would "get ahead of them." You might as well face facts. Some people want to be successful in life, but that does not mean they want someone else to have the same level of success.

Just because someone "has arrived" does not mean they are praying for your "ship to sail in." Just because someone has money does not mean they want you to have one dollar more than what they have. In fact, someone may be counting you out of the "money game" right now before you can even get started. Someone may be counting on you not *following The Infinite Rules To Money*!!!

Frankly, it is your vote in this matter that counts. I am a living witness that the thoughts you hold in the arena of your own mind will determine how wealthy you will be. If you will only dare to go into the privacy of your own mind, where no one else will dare go, and dare to think Infinite Money until it has literally manifested!!!

Here is one last word about this rule: Do not underestimate yourself or the power Of God. In Deuteronomy 8:18, God tells us that it is "He that gives us the power to get wealth, that you might remember that He is the Lord your God." Once you follow these rules, regardless of what others around you are saying and doing, you will get the money you think about, speak about, write about, read about and thank God about!!!

Final Word

Hopefully, you have enjoyed learning about *The Infinite Rules to Money* and how to apply them to your life. Additionally, I hope you are as equally excited as I am about the *Money Harvest* that is just waiting somewhere on the horizon, ready, willing, and able to materialize at any possible second!!!

Just as a farmer cannot expect to receive a harvest if he has not first planted a seed, and just as a farmer should not expect to plant a seed without expecting a harvest, neither can you follow *The Infinite Rules To Money* and not expect a *Money Harvest!!!* The same holds true that you should not expect a *Money Harvest* if you have not followed the rules!!!

The principles and rules contained within this book are seeds that you plant each and every time you endeavor to use them as set forth in this book. Of course, do not be surprised if you discover other principles on your own that are not mentioned in the contents of this book. *The Rules To Money are Infinite!!!*

Just as there are *Infinite Rules To Money*, there are an *Infinite number of ways that* God can put all the *money* you need and want into your physical hands!!! An *Infinite God* wants to put *Infinite Money—Money that just keeps on coming to you—in the power within your reach!!!*

The Infinite Rules To Money In A Glance!!!

Rule # 1: Money Always Goes Where It Is Preached!
Rule # 2: Money Always Goes Where It is Heard!
Rule # 3: Money Always Goes Where It Is Taught!
Rule # 4: Money Always Goes Where It Is Highly Taught!
Rule # 5: Money Always Goes Where It Is Well Spoken Of!
Rule # 6: Money Always Goes Where It Can Be Afforded!
Rule # 7: Money Always Goes Where It Is Studied!
Rule # 8: Money Always Goes Where It Is Expected!
Rule # 9: Money Always Goes Where It Is Blessed!
Rule # 10: Money Always Goes Where It Is Tithed!
Rule # 11: Money Always Goes Where It Can Be Felt!
Rule # 12: Money Always Goes Where It Can Be Seen!
Rule # 13: Money Always Goes Where It Can Be Had!
Rule # 14: Money Always Goes Where It Is Written!
Rule # 15: Money Always Goes Where It Is Wanted!
Rule # 16: Money Always Goes Where It Is Read!
Rule # 17: Money Always Goes Where It Is Welcome!
Rule # 18: Money Always Goes Where It Is Counted!